W9-BTF-402

ULTIMATE COLORING

NATIONAL PARKS

A COLORFUL ADVENTURE INTO THE GREAT OUTDOORS

THUNDER BAY
P · R · E · S · S

San Diego, California

Welcome to *Ultimate Coloring: National Parks*. Turn off your phone and forget the everyday. We're going on a tour of the country, so gather together as many colors as you can find. You're going to need them all.

The national parks of the United States include every type of landscape you can imagine: from ice fields to sand dunes, meadowland to mangroves, mountain ranges, and cave systems. You can see canyons carved by rivers over millions of years, or a log cabin built by settlers not even 200 years ago. Wildflowers bloom after the first spring rain, and there's a pine tree that was already thousands of years old when Brutus helped to kill Julius Caesar. Herds of bison and migrating caribou wander through the parks. Animals endangered elsewhere, such as the black bear or lynx, find sanctuary.

All this is thanks to the National Parks Service, whose purpose is to preserve "the scenery . . . and the wild life therein . . . for future generations." It's been called America's "best idea," and today the Parks Service, which turned 100 years old in 2016, has stewardship of more than 400 areas. Yellowstone was the first national park. The most recent, Pinnacles National Park, was created in 2013.

The Parks Service protects more than 81,000 square miles, both land and sea. Some of this remains unspoiled, as it was before European settlers arrived on the continent. Some of it reveals traces of human activity. These are America's National Parks, and their beauty is yours to enjoy.

YOSEMITE NATIONAL PARK, CALIFORNIA

This World Heritage Site extends across more than 1,100 square miles. Its woodlands, mountains, forests, rivers, and waterfalls are home to endangered animals and rare plants. Its granite rock formations are so spectacular that a newspaper reporter who wrote one of the first descriptions refused to believe it was true. How deep is Yosemite Valley? A full mile.

ACADIA NATIONAL PARK, MAINE

Acadia National Park boasts mountains, evergreen forests, lakes, sandy beaches, rocky beaches, and an ocean coastline. Its beauty has won it support through the years, particularly from the Rockefeller family, who helped to pay for its restoration after a 1947 fire. John D. Rockefeller also funded the construction of roads through the park, guarded along their steep edges by granite stones known as "Rockefeller's Teeth."

CHANNEL ISLANDS NATIONAL PARK, CALIFORNIA

This park comprises five islands off the coast of Southern California. They are isolated and home to animals and plants found nowhere else in the world, earning them the nickname of the "Galapagos of North America." Taking a boat or small plane is the only way to reach the islands, and while there, you'll hike or travel in kayaks to get around.

BRYCE CANYON NATIONAL PARK, UTAH

Nowhere in the world will you find more hoodoos than in Bryce Canyon. Hoodoos are tall, thin spires of rock that can stand up to 150 feet tall. They are formed by the erosion of rock that was laid down in alternating soft and hard layers. As the soft rock eroded, the hard rock remained, creating pillars of varying thicknesses. In Bryce Canyon, water seeping into the cracks in the winter freezes and expands, accelerating the process.

GRAND CANYON NATIONAL PARK, ARIZONA

Grand Canyon National Park, a World Heritage Site, covers more than 1,900 square miles, and the gorge from which it takes its name was six million years in the making. At least a mile deep, up to 18 miles wide, and 277 miles long, it was carved out by the Colorado River. Theodore Roosevelt said of the Grand Canyon, "It is beyond comparison—beyond description," and urged every American to see it.

CRATER LAKE NATIONAL PARK, OREGON

At the center of this national park is Crater Lake, the deepest lake in the United States. No river flows into or out of it, so rain and snowfall maintain the famously blue, clear water, which is also among the purest in the world. Snow covers the park for up to eight months of the year to depths of about 15 feet.

KENAI FJORDS NATIONAL PARK, ALASKA

On Alaska's Kenai Peninsula stands a national park that contains most of the Harding Icefield, the largest in the United States. The icefield receives more than 400 inches of snow each year and spawns glaciers that carve their way down the mountains, creating the many fjords that give the park its name. Expect to see humpback, minke, and killer whales in the water, and black bears and moose on land.

OLYMPIC NATIONAL PARK, WASHINGTON

Situated on a peninsula bordered by a mountain range, the land that is now this national park holds more than 500 square miles of forests. In fact, the area was designated a national park in 1938 partly to protect both the forest and the Roosevelt elk that live among the trees. Even today, logging remains a hot topic as related to this park.

SAGUARO NATIONAL PARK, ARIZONA

Established to protect the giant saguaro cactus, this park is also home to many other species. These include several types of cholla cactus (staghorn, teddybear, and chainfruit), the pinkflower hedgehog cactus, and the prickly pear cactus. Conserving large tracts of desert, this park is also home to desert wildlife, many of whom depend on the saguaro: hawks nest in its arms, bats feed on its nectar, and jackrabbits and deer eat its flesh when water is scarce.

ARCHES NATIONAL PARK, UTAH

At this park, more than 2,000 natural sandstone arches stand in an area of less than 120 square miles. They were formed by erosion caused by an annual rainfall of 8 to 10 inches, which is enough to soak into the sandstone and slowly dissolve it, but not so much that the rock erodes too quickly for arches to form. The process is ongoing: since 1977 at least forty-three arches have collapsed as others continue to grow.

GLACIER NATIONAL PARK, MONTANA

What makes Glacier National Park so remarkable is that it has remained mostly untouched. The European settlers who so changed the continent had virtually no impact on this area. Grizzly bears, wolverines, and the Canadian lynx are rare in other parts of the United States, but all make their homes here. The glaciers that give the park its name are retreating fast, however; only 25 remain, from an estimated 150 in the 19th century.

ZION NATIONAL PARK, UTAH

Located where the Mojave Desert meets the Colorado Plateau and the Great Basin, Zion National Park includes mountains, rivers, canyons, mesas, deserts, and forests. These landscapes support more than a thousand species of plants, from pines to prickly pears, which in turn support a variety of wildlife, such as toads, mountain lions, rattlesnakes, and flycatchers. The California condor, endangered elsewhere, breeds successfully here.

THEODORE ROOSEVELT NATIONAL PARK, NORTH DAKOTA

The North Dakota badlands are an austere landscape that attracts relatively few visitors. Here you can see bison, elk, and the Nakota horse, a wild breed that almost vanished during the early 1900s. When the park was established in the 1940s, the few remaining bands of Nakota horses had a safe home. How appropriate for a park that was created to honor the president who did so much to promote conservation in the United States.

YELLOWSTONE NATIONAL PARK, WYOMING

The first U.S. national park is perhaps best known for its many geysers, including Old Faithful. But hot springs, mud pools, and steam vents (or fumaroles) all bear witness to the ongoing volcanic activity underneath Yellowstone. The springs and the channels in the park are often brightly colored, thanks to minerals in the water, bacteria, or algae. Expect to see emerald greens, yellows, oranges, and even reds.

ISLE ROYALE NATIONAL PARK, MICHIGAN

Isle Royale and the 400 islands surrounding it constitute a national park within Lake Superior. Isolated by water, Isle Royale is a unique environment: there are far fewer mammal species here than on the mainland. Some wolves crossed from Ontario via an ice bridge during the harsh winter of 1949, and moose swam the lake in the early 1900s. No one knows how the red squirrel arrived, however.

ROCKY MOUNTAIN NATIONAL PARK, COLORADO

Ninety-five percent of this park is designated wilderness. Grasslands appear at lower elevations (around 7,600 feet). At higher elevations (around 14,250 feet), there are icefields and small glaciers. Pine and fir trees cover the mountains, while aspens grow alongside streams. Such a range of ecosystems means that the park is home to a variety of wildlife, including bighorn sheep, black bears, snowshoe hares, and mule deer.

MAMMOTH CAVE NATIONAL PARK, KENTUCKY

Why "mammoth"? Because this is the longest cave system in the world. So far, about 400 miles of passageways have been explored, and some geologists believe that the entire system may be 1,000 miles long. Cave guides offer tours. Bats have lived in the caves for millions of years, but today their numbers are low, and some species are endangered.

GREAT SMOKY MOUNTAINS NATIONAL PARK, NORTH CAROLINA/TENNESSEE

Straddling the border of Tennessee and North Carolina is a park that is almost all forest—pine, oak, spruce, fir, hemlock, beech, maple, dogwood, and magnolia. More than one-third is old growth, meaning it predates the arrival of European settlers. The park is also home to many black bears.

EVERGLADES NATIONAL PARK, FLORIDA

The Florida Everglades make up North America's largest tropical wetlands, which is home to a wide variety of plants and animals. These include Florida panthers, crocodiles, West Indian manatees, alligators, herons, and numerous others. Although it looks static, the Everglades is actually a slow-moving river that flows for more than 100 miles.

GRAND TETON NATIONAL PARK, WYOMING

Log cabins built by nineteenth-century homesteaders still stand in Grand Teton National Park. The low-lying valleys surrounded by high mountains seemed to offer settlers good opportunities, but harsh weather and rocky soils prove challenging. Instead, it was fur trappers who thrived—the region's many rivers and streams meant that beavers were particularly plentiful. Today visitors can walk the same trails created by the trappers.

MOUNT RAINIER NATIONAL PARK, WASHINGTON

Mount Rainier, an active volcano south of Seattle, climbs to more than 14,000 feet and is covered with snow and glacial ice. Across the region, from meadow to rainforest to mountain, wildflowers thrive. Those on the mountain are perhaps the most spectacular. Snow often lingers into the summer, and the short growing season means they bloom profusely.

CHACO CULTURE NATIONAL HISTORICAL PARK, NEW MEXICO

This park is home to the most densely built group of Native American pueblos in the United States. These huge, multi-story buildings, created between AD 850 and 1150, are the mark of a sophisticated culture. Not until the nineteenth century were structures of a similar size built in North America. So what forced the Ancient Pueblo Peoples who created them to abandon the area? Climate change. A drought began around 1130 and lasted for fifty years, forcing them to move on.

CUMBERLAND GAP NATIONAL PARK, KENTUCKY/TENNESSEE/VIRGINIA

The Cumberland Gap is a natural break in the Appalachian Mountains chain. Bison and deer used the route for migration, which made it a good hunting territory for Native Americans. From the late eighteenth century, Cumberland Gap was the route for pioneers moving west. In the early 1900s, a small community developed, peaking at around a hundred people by 1925. The log cabins and one-room schoolhouse have been preserved.

SEQUOIA & KINGS CANYON NATIONAL PARK, CALIFORNIA

The giant sequoias that give this park its name grow to be as tall as 275 feet and can live for up to 3,000 years. The landscape gives visitors a sense of what the Sierra Nevada region was like before the arrival of European settlers. Mild winters and summers offer ideal growing conditions, and a high concentration of tannin in their bark makes the sequoias resistant to rot, insects, and fire.

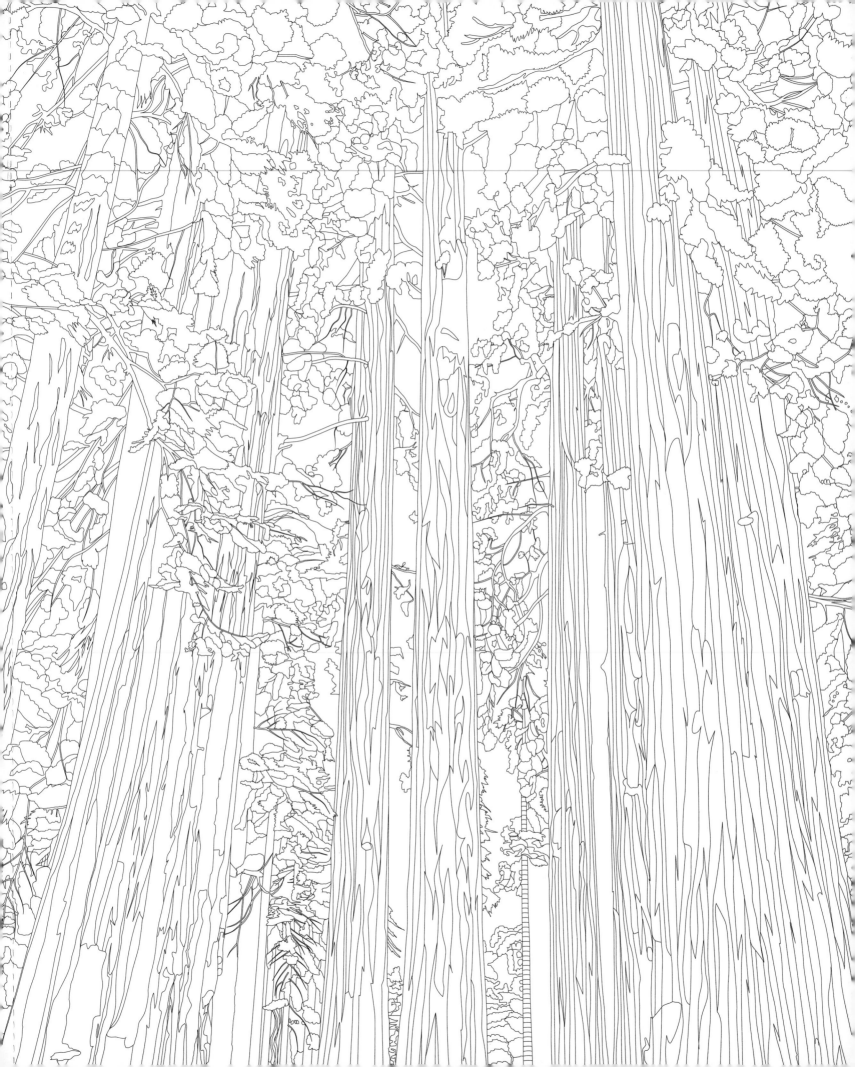

MESA VERDE NATIONAL PARK, COLORADO

Mesa Verde is a significant archaeological site. Nomadic Paleo-Indians passed through here as early as 9500 BC, and the first structures date from around AD 600. There are around 5,000 sites of interest, including 600 cliff dwellings, many of which are incredibly well-preserved. The Ancestral Puebloans were farmers who built dams and reservoirs, and it seems that a decades-long drought forced them to emigrate away from the settlements during the thirteenth century, leaving the area almost completely uninhabited.

SHENANDOAH NATIONAL PARK, VIRGINIA

When it was established in 1935, Shenandoah was a place where people had lived for more than a century. Most of the families on this land in the Blue Ridge Mountains were farmers, and even though conditions could be harsh, many were reluctant to move. Today cemeteries are the most visible reminders of those now vanished communities, as forests have returned, erasing the signs of farming and logging.

CANYONLANDS NATIONAL PARK, UTAH

Canyonlands National Park boasts spectacular canyons, arches, and pinnacles. There are also extraordinary carvings, some of them 2,000 years old. Pictures of deer and buffalo sit alongside images of riders on horseback, carefully inscribed into the "desert varnish," a black deposit formed on sandstone by bacteria and rainwater that has been carefully cut away to reveal the lighter rock beneath.

LAKE CLARK NATIONAL PARK & PRESERVE, ALASKA

Boat or small plane is the only way to reach this park, where Alaska's diverse landscape awaits: glaciers, volcanoes, lakes, coasts, forests, and tundra. Both grizzlies and black bears roam the park, attracted to the salmon spawning in rivers and creeks. So plentiful, in fact, are the sockeye salmon in this area that a pack of wolves at Lake Clark is the only one in the world known to depend on salmon for food.

REDWOOD NATIONAL AND STATE PARKS, CALIFORNIA

The seed of a redwood is the same size as that of a tomato, but from it will grow a tree that may be 350 feet tall and can live for more than 500 years. (Some live to be 2,000 years old.) Redwoods have been growing along the coast of northern California for 20 million years, and today they grow nowhere else. This park protects almost half of the redwoods left in the state.

KOBUK VALLEY NATIONAL PARK, ALASKA

The Kobuk Valley is well known for the herd of caribou, nearly half a million strong, that migrates through it twice a year. The Onion Portage, where the caribou swim across the Kobuk River, is now a National Historic Landmark. Today the local Iñupiat people continue to hunt the caribou here, as they have done for 9,000 years.

NORTH CASCADES NATIONAL PARK, WASHINGTON

The North Cascades are sometimes called the American Alps, and in the spring and summer, wildflowers are everywhere. They crawl along the floor of old-growth forests and bloom in alpine meadows. Today more than 90 percent of the park is wilderness. The area is also home to a variety of wildlife, including Canadian elk, gray wolves, and grizzly bears.

DRY TORTUGAS NATIONAL PARK, FLORIDA

About 70 miles west of Key West stands Dry Tortugas National Park, which preserves a seven-island archipelago and its magnificent coral reefs. Expect to see angelfish, parrotfish, and moray eels, and in the summer, turtles return to bury their eggs. Also preserved is Fort Jefferson, an unfinished fortress that served as a prison during the mid 1800s and, at one time, held four men who conspired to assassinate President Abraham Lincoln. Today it offers great opportunities for bird watching, as many migratory birds pass through.

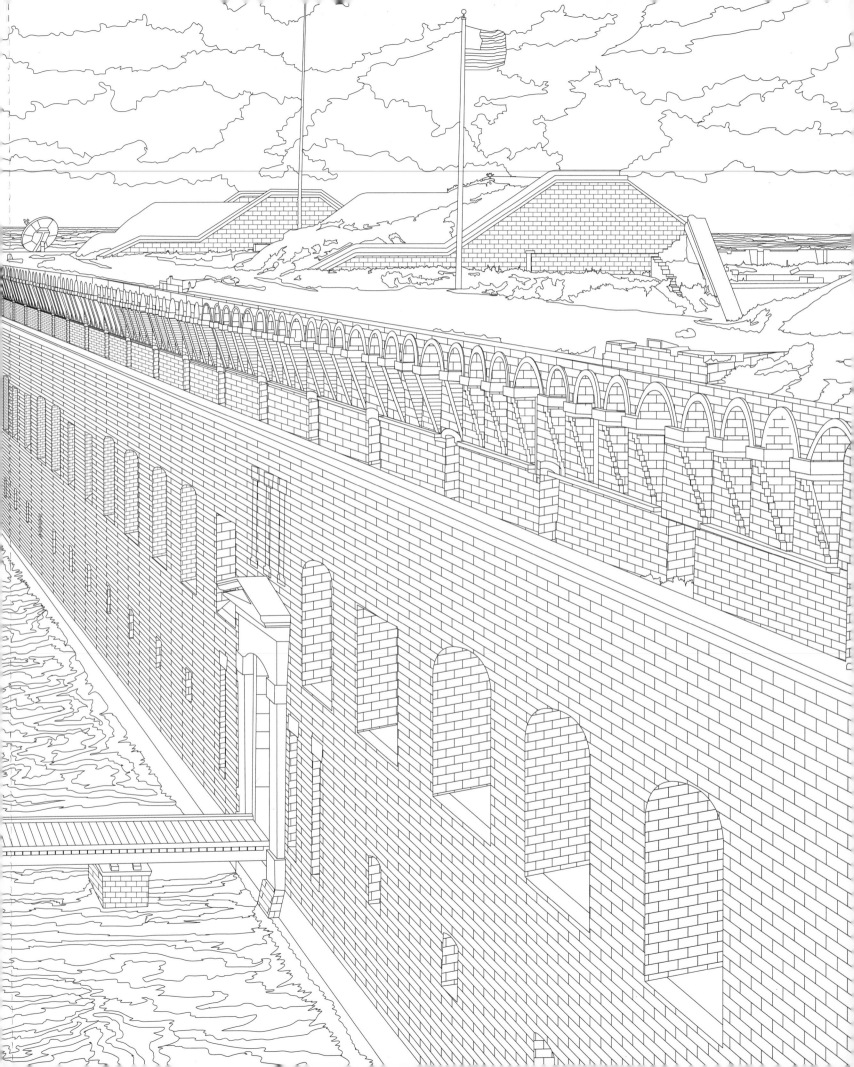

GREAT BASIN NATIONAL PARK, NEVADA

Great Basin National Park is best known for its many bristlecone pines. These are trees that thrive in poor environments where other plants struggle, such as alkaline soil or in regions with very little rain. Bristlecone pines can live for up to 5,000 years, and their wood is so dense that dead trees do not rot. Instead, they remain standing and erode as stone does, via the action of wind and rain.

CONGAREE NATIONAL PARK, SOUTH CAROLINA

This park preserves old-growth bottomland hardwood forest, which grows in floodplains and can resist flooding—that happens up to ten times a year here. Established in 2003, the park exists largely thanks to conservationists who resisted the threat of logging, and it is now classified as a Globally Important Bird Area. Woodpeckers can be heard hard at work during the day, and at night in the spring and fall, rangers lead "owl prowls" to hear the calls of barred owls.

GUADALUPE MOUNTAINS
NATIONAL PARK, TEXAS

One of the least-known parks in the country, this one lies in the Guadalupe Mountains of West Texas. The park includes salt flats and creosote deserts; canyons with maple, ash, and beech trees; and alpine uplands blanketed with pines, fir, and aspen. Springs of water enable trees to grow in this desert region, while some wildflowers bloom after monsoon rains.

BLACK CANYON OF THE GUNNISON NATIONAL PARK, COLORADO

It took about two million years for the Gunnison River to carve its way through the rock and create this canyon. The name comes not from the color of the stone, which is dark gray, but from the gorge itself. It is so steep in places that it stands in darkness for most of the day. Sunlight reaches into the gorge only at midday, and then for barely more than half an hour.

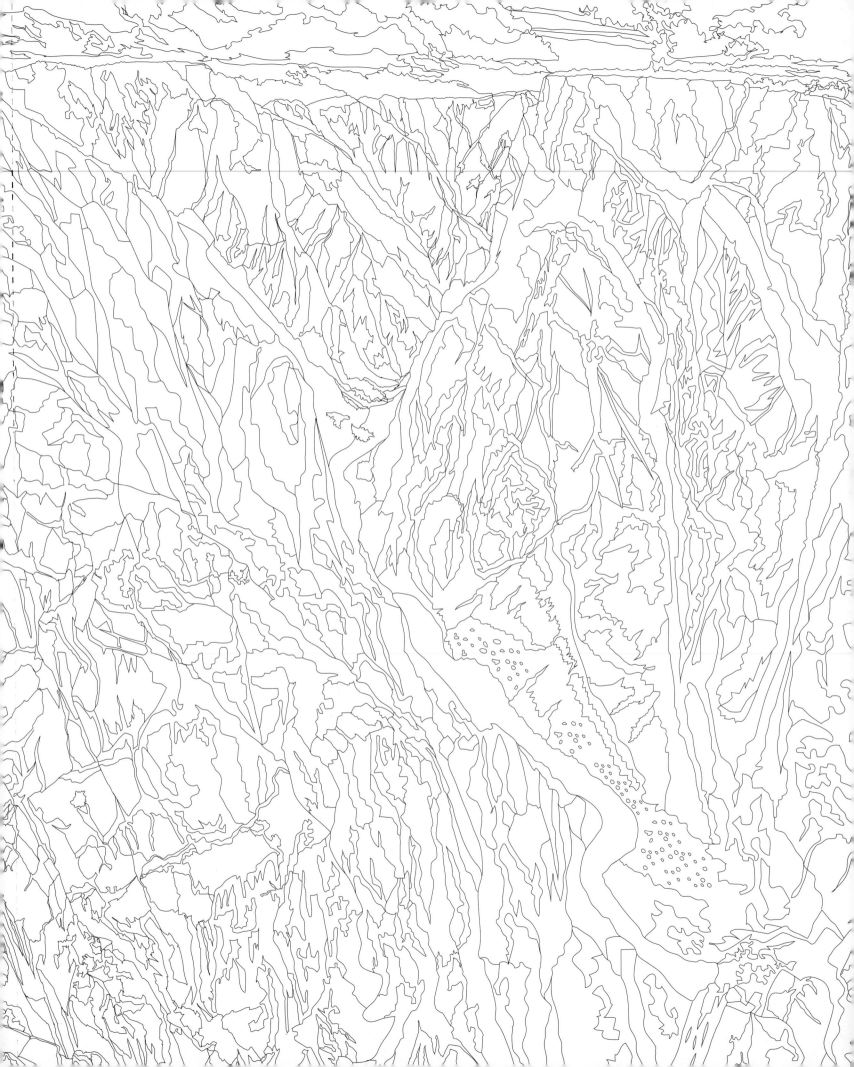

BISCAYNE NATIONAL PARK, FLORIDA

Biscayne National Park is 95 percent water. It includes an extensive mangrove forest and Biscayne Bay, a lagoon about 10 feet deep. Mangroves offer a nursery for fish and crustacean larvae, and also shelter crabs, fish, and wading birds. The shallow waters of the lagoon support diving birds such as cormorants, as well as manatees and bottlenose dolphins.

CAPITOL REEF NATIONAL PARK, UTAH

Capitol Reef was established to preserve its geological formations. To the west lie layers of rock around 270 million years old; those to the east are "only" 80 million years old. In the rocks, visitors can see different layers that show where rivers and seas flowed during the Permian Period, where deserts lay during the Triassic, and where volcanoes were active in the Cretaceous. This is a landscape that makes visible Earth's long history.

WRANGELL-ST. ELIAS
NATIONAL PARK & PRESERVE,
ALASKA

Inside Wrangell-St. Elias National Park stands the abandoned mining town of Kennecott. For thirty years, until 1938, it produced copper ore, but as the highest grade was depleted, the mines closed. All that's left now is a ghost town. With the exception of the hospital, the buildings in Kennecott were all painted red, simply because that was the cheapest color of paint at the time.

WIND CAVE NATIONAL PARK, SOUTH DAKOTA

This park is small, little more than 44 square miles, but it is home to a herd of bison that has never bred with domestic cattle, one of only four such herds in North America. The park also includes the largest mixed-grass natural prairie left, and that is where visitors generally see the bison, though in the summer they stay close to the forests so they can get shade.

JEAN LAFITTE NATIONAL HISTORICAL PARK & PRESERVE, LOUISIANA

Experience the unique environment of the Mississippi River Delta while you can. Rising sea levels mean that the Louisiana coastline is disappearing fast—an area the size of a football field washes away every thirty minutes. This means that the wetlands in this park, home to more than 200 species of birds, are now under threat. Currently, there are trails that lead visitors through the park's forests, swamps, and marshes.

PETRIFIED FOREST NATIONAL PARK, ARIZONA

Known for fossilized trees dating back to the Late Triassic Period, about 225 million years ago, the park also gives us a glimpse of the animals that roamed the area during the age of the dinosaurs. Fossils of early dinosaurs, amphibians, and giant reptiles have been found throughout the park. Today, you'll find salamanders, toads, and nine kinds of lizards. Preying on scorpions, spiders, and small mammals, these lizards are an important part of the park's ecosystem.

LASSEN VOLCANIC NATIONAL PARK, CALIFORNIA

Fly-fishers from across the United States come to Manzanita Lake, which is home to brown and rainbow trout. Reflected in those waters is Lassen Peak, a volcano that was dormant for about 27,000 years. Then in 1915, the mountain exploded, an event that could be seen from 150 miles away. The volcano is active to this day, but parts of it are covered permanently in snow, thanks to 660 inches falling each year.

GREAT SAND DUNES NATIONAL PARK & PRESERVE, COLORADO

The sand dunes in this park stand so high (750 feet) because they are constantly evolving. Two mountain streams flow alongside the dunes, picking up sand and carrying it to the grasslands. From there, the water drains into the land, leaving the wind to pick up the sand and blow it back to the dunes. On windy days, visitors can experience the process for themselves.

VOYAGEURS NATIONAL PARK, MINNESOTA

Voyageurs (meaning "travelers" in French) pays tribute to the French Canadian fur traders who were the first Europeans to journey through this area. They came by water in birch-bark canoes, and access to the park today is still mainly by water. The park incorporates all or part of four major lakes, three of which straddle the border with Canada, and there are more than 340 square miles of water for visitors to enjoy.

PINNACLES NATIONAL PARK, CALIFORNIA

This landscape was created nearly 23 million years ago by a series of volcanic eruptions. They took place about 200 miles to the southeast, and tremors in the San Andreas Fault carried the rock formations here. The spectacular pinnacles that give the park its name were formed from those rocks by erosion. Today the United States Geological Survey continues to monitor seismic activity in the park.

Thunder Bay Press
An imprint of Printers Row Publishing Group
10350 Barnes Canyon Road, Suite 100, San Diego, CA 92121
www.thunderbaybooks.com

Copyright © 2016 Carlton Books Limited

All rights reserved. No part of this publication may be reproduced, distributed, or transmitted in any form or by any means, including photocopying, recording, or other electronic or mechanical methods, without the prior written permission of the publisher, except in the case of brief quotations embodied in critical reviews and certain other noncommercial uses permitted by copyright law.

Printers Row Publishing Group is a division of Readerlink Distribution Services, LLC. Thunder Bay Press is a registered trademark of Readerlink Distribution Services, LLC.

All notations of errors or omissions should be addressed to Thunder Bay Press, Editorial Department, at the above address. All other correspondence (author inquiries, permissions) concerning the content of this book should be addressed to Carlton Books Ltd, 20 Mortimer Street, London W1T 3JW
www.carltonbooks.co.uk

Thunder Bay Press
Publisher: Peter Norton
Associate Publisher: Ana Parker
Publishing/Editorial Team: Kathryn C. Dalby, April Farr, Kelly Larsen
Editorial Team: JoAnn Padgett, Melinda Allman

ISBN: 978-1-62686-844-1

Printed in China

22 21 20 19 3 4 5 6

The publishers would like to thank the following sources for their kind permission to reproduce the pictures in this book.
3. Steve Broer/Shutterstock.com, 5. Edwin Remsberg/Getty Images, 7. Mint Images - Frans Lanting/Getty Images, 9. David Sucsy/Getty Images, 11. Sumikophoto/Getty Images, 13. Lynn Wegener/Design Pics/Getty Images, 15. Visuals Unlimited, Inc./Ellen Bishop/Getty Images, 17. Danita Delimont/Getty Images, 19. Galyna Andrushko/Shutterstock.com, 21. Anton Foltin/Shutterstock.com, 23. Danita Delimont/Getty Images, 25. BGSmith/Shutterstock.com, 27. Andrew S/Shutterstock.com, 29. Stephen Saks/Getty Images, 31. Kris Wiktor/Shutterstock.com, 33. Posnov/Getty Images, 35. Drewthehobbit/Shutterstock.com, 37. Danita Delimont/Getty Images, 39. Danita Delimont/Getty Images, 41. Radius Images/Getty Images, 43. Jeffrey B. Banke/Shutterstock.com, 45. Danita Delimont/Getty Images, 47. Zack Frank/Shutterstock.com, 49. Danita Delimont/Getty Images, 51. Ladislav Pavliha/iStockphoto.com, 53. Nagel Photography/Shutterstock.com, 55. Design Pics/Bilderbuch/Getty Images, 57. Scott Prokop/Shutterstock.com, 59. Richard Garvey-Williams/NIS/Minden Pictures, 61. Zack Frank/Shutterstock.com, 63. Nick Jans/Alaska Stock, 65. Alan Majchrowicz/Getty Images, 67. Steven Frame/Alamy Stock Photo, 69. Rob Blakers/Getty Images, 71. Natalia Bratslavsky/Shutterstock.com, 73. Witold Skrypczak/Getty Images, 75. Alexey Kamenskiy/Shutterstock.com, 77. Tom Stack/Alamy Stock Photo, 79. Victor Maschek/Shutterstock.com, 81. Benny Marty/Shutterstock.com, 83. S.J. Krasemann/Getty Images, 85. Danita Delimont/Getty Images, 87. robertharding/Alamy Stock Photo, 89. Ron Thomas/iStockphoto.com, 91. Kris Wiktor/Shutterstock.com, 93. Don Breneman/Alamy Stock Photo, 95. Mike Brake/Shutterstock.com, 96. Edwin Remsberg/Getty Images
Every effort has been made to acknowledge correctly and contact the source and/or copyright holder of each picture, and Carlton Books Limited apologizes for any unintentional errors or omissions, which will be corrected in future editions.